Color my Penis!
BY
ann Huey
12 Twat-Tinglers to Color and Mount (on your wall!)

© ann Huey
BLOWman

HaPPeNiS
© ann Huey

THE
Enchanted
PHALLUS

© ANN HUEY
Peenies from Heaven

©ANN HUEY
Earthly
Garden
Delights

THE Unihorn
Believe

©ann Huey
THE
Foreskin of July

© Ann Hucy
COCKLE SHELLS

Psychedelick

HAPPY!
HALLOWEENIE
HAPPY!
HAPPY
HAPPY!

La Petite
Fresh from The Oven
Ann Huey

O, horny night

HAPPY
BANG!
KA-BOOM!
POP!
SQUEAL!
©ann Huey

www.ingramcontent.com/pod-product-compliance
Lightning Source LLC
Chambersburg PA
CBHW051833210526
45473CB00005B/1852
9781986450935